# Banner Blitz: Mastering the Art of Advertising with Eye-Catching Banners

B. Vincent

Published by RWG Publishing, 2023.

BANNER BLITZ: MASTERING THE ART OF ADVERTISING WITH EYE-CATCHING BANNERS

**First edition. April 4, 2023.**

Written by B. Vincent.

# Also by B. Vincent

**Affiliate Marketing**
Affiliate Marketing
Affiliate Marketing

**Standalone**
Business Employee Discipline
Affiliate Recruiting
Business Layoffs & Firings
Business and Entrepreneur Guide
Business Remote Workforce
Career Transition
Project Management
Precision Targeting
Professional Development
Strategic Planning
Content Marketing
Imminent List Building
Getting Past GateKeepers
Banner Ads
Bookkeeping
Bridge Pages
Business Acquisition

Business Bogging
Business Communication Course
Marketing Automation
Better Meetings
Business Conflict Resolution
Business Culture Course
Conversion Optimization
Creative Solutions
Employee Recruitment
Startup Capital
Employee Incentives
Employee Mentoring
Followership
Servant Leadership
Human Resources
Team Building
Freelancing
Funnel Building
Geo Targeting
Goal Setting
Immanent List Building
Lead Generation
Leadership Course
Leadership Transition
Leadership vs Management
LinkedIn Ads
LinkedIn Marketing
Messenger Marketing
New Management
Newsfeed Ads
Search Ads
Online Learning
Sales Webinars

Side Hustles

Split Testing

Twitter Timeline Advertising

Earning Additional Income Through Side Hustles: Begin Earning Money Immediately

Making a Living Through Blogging: Earn Money Working From Home

Create Bonuses for Affiliate Marketing: Your Success Is Encompassed by Your Bonuses

Internet Marketing Success: The Most Effective Traffic-Driving Strategies

JV Recruiting: Joint Ventures Partnerships and Affiliates

Secrets to List Building

Step-by-Step Facebook Marketing: Discover How To Create A Strategy That Will Help You Grow Your Business

Banner Advertising: Traffic Can Be Boosted by Banner Ads

Affiliate Marketing

Improve Your Marketing Strategy with Internet Marketing

Outsourcing Helps You Save Time and Money

Choosing the Right Content and Marketing for Social Media

Make Products That Will Sell

Launching a Product for Affiliate Marketing

Pinterest as a Marketing Tool

Banner Blitz: Mastering the Art of Advertising with Eye-Catching Banners

# Table of Contents

# Chapter 1: The Power of Visual Advertising: Understanding the Role of Banners

———

Visual advertising is more crucial than it has ever been in today's fast-paced world. People are constantly being inundated with information, making it difficult to leave an impression that will stick with them. Banners are a fantastic tool for capturing people's attention and making an impression that will stick with them. In this chapter, we will discuss the effectiveness of visual advertising as well as the ways in which banners can be an important component of your overall marketing strategy.

The goal of all visual advertising is to elicit an emotional response from the target audience. You want people to feel something, whether you're trying to sell a product, promote a service, or simply raise awareness of an issue. This should be your goal. Banners are used for this purpose at this point. Banners are a versatile form of visual advertising that can be hung in a number of different locations. They may also be displayed in physical locations, such as trade shows and other events, in addition to websites and social media platforms.

Banners can be used for a variety of purposes, which is one of the many reasons why they are so useful. Banners can be made to fit any size or shape, and they can be used in a wide variety of different environments. For instance, you might make a banner that is tailored specifically for use on social media by giving it a certain aspect ratio and designing it in a way that conforms to the aesthetic of the platform. You could also make a banner that is intended to be displayed in a physical location. This type of banner would be significantly larger and feature a more eye-catching design.

Banners offer a number of benefits, one of which is the ability to direct them toward particular audiences. This is significant because not all forms of advertising are applicable to each and every person. You can increase the likelihood of reaching the appropriate people by tailoring your banners to specific demographics or interest groups and distributing them online. This has the potential to result in higher engagement rates and improved outcomes.

When designing a banner, it is essential to keep in mind the fundamentals of good graphic design. Balance, contrast, and hierarchy are all aspects that fall under this category. By adhering to these guidelines, you'll be able to design a banner that is not only visually appealing but also effective at conveying the message you want to convey. You could, for instance, use colors that contrast with one another to draw attention to important aspects of your banner. Alternatively, you could use hierarchy to prioritize the information that is most pertinent to your audience.

There are design principles that should be followed, but there are also best practices that should be followed when making effective banners. These include things like utilizing images of a high quality, ensuring that the text is concise and gets right to the point, and including a call to action in the content. A statement that encourages people to take a particular action, such as clicking on a link or making a purchase, is referred to as a "call to action." You can improve your chances of converting viewers into customers by including a call to action in the banner that you are displaying on your website.

Last but not least, it is essential that you evaluate how successful your banners have been. Utilizing analytics tools that keep track of things like impressions, clicks, and conversions is one way to accomplish this goal.

Through the examination of these data, you will be able to determine which banners are successful and which ones have room for advancement. This can assist you in improving the efficiency of your advertising efforts and bringing in more business over time.

To summarize, banners are an effective method for presenting graphical advertising. You can design banners that are not only visually appealing but also successful in conveying your message if you have an understanding of the design principles, follow the best practices, and measure the effectiveness of your efforts. Banners are a great way to reach your audience and leave an impression that will stick with them, whether you're trying to promote a product, service, or cause.

# Chapter 2: From Boring to Bold: Transforming Your Banner Designs

———

Do your banner designs feel stale and uninspired? Do you find it difficult to make banners that distinguish themselves from the other participants? In the following section, we will discuss how to give your banner designs a more daring and exciting appearance.

To begin the process of transforming your banner designs, the first thing you need to do is think creatively. Experimenting with new ideas and methods of operation should be prioritized over relying on the tried-and-true components of design. This may include the use of striking typography, the incorporation of one-of-a-kind illustrations, or the experimentation with nontraditional color palettes. The objective is to design a banner that is both attention-grabbing and easy to recall.

Putting the emphasis on the user experience is yet another method for transforming your banner designs. To accomplish this, banners need to be designed so that they are simple to read, navigate, and interact with. This could involve utilizing messaging that is straightforward and to the point, incorporating interactive elements such as buttons or sliders, or optimizing for mobile devices. You can make banners that are not only visually appealing but also effective at achieving your marketing goals if you center your efforts on the experience of the people who will be viewing them.

Utilizing the most recent design trends is yet another method you can use to transform the designs of your banners. Incorporating elements such as gradients, 3D typography, or geometric shapes could be one way to accomplish this goal. You will be able to design banners that have a contemporary and contemporary feel to them if you keep up with the latest design trends.

The content of your banners should be given careful consideration in addition to the design elements that go into them. Are you able to convey your message in an effective manner? Are you communicating with your target audience using language and messaging that strikes a chord with them? You can increase the number of people who engage with and respond to your banners by developing content that is compelling.

In conclusion, it is essential to keep in mind that the design of a banner is an iterative process. This indicates that you should continually put your designs through rigorous testing and make adjustments to them based on the feedback and information you receive. You can determine what works and what doesn't by putting different design elements and messaging to the test. This will allow you to optimize your designs for the greatest possible impact.

In conclusion, in order to transform your banner designs from dull to bold, you will need to combine creativity, user experience, and data-driven optimization. You can create banners that are visually appealing and effective at achieving your marketing goals by experimenting with new ideas and approaches, focusing on the user experience, tapping into current design trends, crafting compelling content, and continually testing and refining your designs. If you do all of these things, you will be able to create banners.

# Chapter 3: The Anatomy of an Eye-Catching Banner

---

What characteristics define an arresting banner? In this chapter, we will examine the structure of a banner and identify the components that must be present in order to make a banner that successfully attracts people's attention.

The headline is the primary component that makes a banner interesting to look at. The headline ought to be succinct and catchy, and it should convey the primary message that the banner is trying to convey. Even from a considerable distance, the headline ought to be easily readable and obvious to the reader. The font ought to be of a size that allows it to be read without difficulty, and its color ought to contrast with the background.

The visual is the second component that makes up an attention-grabbing banner. The visual ought to be captivating and pertinent to the message that the banner is trying to convey. It is important that the visual be of a high-quality, with a high resolution and crystal clear. In addition to this, the visual should not contain any clutter or distracting elements and should be straightforward and easy to comprehend. The image ought to capture the viewer's attention and entice them to look further into the banner.

The call to action constitutes the third component of an attention-grabbing banner. The viewer should be told clearly and specifically what action they should take in response to the call to action, which should be as clear and specific as possible. It is important that the call to action be clear and easy to spot, and that it be repeated multiple times across the banner, especially in the final portion. The phrase that serves as the "call to action" ought to be formulated in such a way that it generates a feeling of either urgency or excitement.

The brand logo is the fourth component that makes up an attention-grabbing banner. The brand's logo ought to be noticeable and easy to spot, but it shouldn't be dominant. It is important that the brand logo be placed on the banner in such a way that it does not detract from the message being communicated. It is important that the brand logo be designed in a way that makes it simple to recognize and easy to recall.

The color scheme is the fifth component of an eye-catching banner that should be considered. It is important that the color scheme be attractive and visually appealing, in addition to being consistent with the identity of the brand. It is important to choose the color scheme with care, taking into consideration the psychology of color and the ways in which different colors can elicit different feelings and responses from a person.

The layout is the sixth component of an attention-grabbing banner that should be considered. The structure ought to be straightforward and uncomplicated to comprehend, with a distinct informational hierarchy. The layout ought to be balanced and aesthetically pleasing, with plenty of white space to help the important elements stand out and draw attention to themselves. It is important that the layout be optimized for the medium on which the banner will be displayed, whether that medium is a website, social media platform, or some other physical location.

In conclusion, the headline, visual, call to action, brand logo, color scheme, and layout are the components that comprise the anatomy of an attention-grabbing banner. You can create banners that get people's attention and effectively communicate your message if you pay attention to these elements and design banners that are visually appealing, simple to understand, and optimized for the platform. This will allow you to create banners that are effective in communicating your message.

# Chapter 4: Crafting Your Message: Tips for Writing Effective Ad Copy

———

The written content that you include in your banner advertisements is of equal significance to the visual components. In this chapter, we will discuss some helpful hints for writing persuasive advertisement copy that will attract the attention of your target audience and encourage them to take action.

The first piece of advice for writing compelling advertisement copy is to keep it succinct and to the point. Because there is only a limited amount of space available, banner ads require that every word count. Concentrate on conveying your message in the most understandable and succinct manner possible. When communicating with your audience, use simple vocabulary and concise sentences to avoid confusing or overwhelming them.

The second piece of advice is to center your attention not on the features, but on the benefits. People are more interested in the benefits that a product or service will provide for them as opposed to the specifics of how it will work. Instead of focusing on the features of your product or service, you should emphasize how it will help customers solve a problem or make their lives easier. Make use of language that plays to their feelings and satisfies their needs.

The third piece of advice is to always speak in an active voice. When compared to passive voice, active voice is more interesting to the reader and requires less effort. Additionally, it exudes an air of self-assurance and authority. Therefore, it is more accurate to say that "Our customers love our product" rather than "Our product is loved by our customers." Even though it's a minor adjustment, it might have a significant impact.

The utilization of power words is the fourth piece of advice. Words that elicit strong feelings and generate a sense of urgency or excitement are referred to as power words. People can be effectively motivated to take action by phrases such as "limited time offer," "exclusive," and "new and improved," among other similar phrases. Make strategic use of power words, but avoid using them too frequently because they can lose their impact if they are utilized too frequently.

The use of numbers and statistics is the fifth piece of advice. Claims that are supported by data are more likely to be accepted as true by the general public. Therefore, if you have evidence in the form of statistics or data to back up your claims, be sure to include it in the text of your advertisement. As an illustration, rather than claiming that "Our product is the best on the market," you could say that "Over 90% of our customers say that our product is the best on the market."

Being specific is the sixth piece of advice. Instead of using generalizations, use specific details that will assist your audience in better comprehending exactly what it is that you are providing for them. For instance, you could say "Save 20% on our product when you buy it today" rather than "Get a great deal on our product," which would be more accurate.

The use of a conversational tone is the seventh piece of advice. People are more likely to interact with content that seems to originate from a real person, as opposed to a nameless and faceless corporation. Therefore, it is important to use language that sounds normal and conversational, and to avoid using language that is overly formal or technical.

The eighth piece of advice is to zero in on a single central message. Do not make the mistake of trying to include an excessive amount of information in your banner ad. Instead, zero in on a single point of communication or a specific call to action. Your advertisement copy will benefit from this by becoming more focused and easier to understand.

In conclusion, writing advertising copy that is effective requires a combination of clear communication, emotional appeal, and language that is persuasive. You can create banner ads that are engaging, persuasive, and effective at motivating people to take action by keeping your copy short and sweet, focusing on benefits, using active voice, using power words, using numbers and statistics, being specific, using a conversational tone, and focusing on a single message. In addition, you should keep your copy focused on a single message.

# Chapter 5: The Dos and Don'ts of Banner Design

———

Creating a banner from scratch can be a difficult undertaking. There are a lot of different things to think about, and it's simple to make mistakes that could end up having a negative effect on how well your banner works. In this chapter, we will discuss the dos and don'ts of banner design, which will allow you to design banners that are not only effective but also have a polished and professional appearance.

DO: Keep it simple. Since banner ads only have a certain amount of space, it is essential to keep the design straightforward and concentrated. Only include in your design those components that are absolutely necessary to effectively convey your message. Keep in mind that complexity and clutter, both of which can be overwhelming and distracting, should be avoided.

DON'T: Overcomplicate your design. You should fight the urge to add an excessive number of design elements or to make your banner too complicated. This may result in misunderstandings and a message that is not as clear as it could be. Maintain a straightforward and uncomplicated layout, and place your emphasis on a select few key components that will both pique the interest of your target audience and effectively convey the meaning of your message.

DO: Make sure to use a font that is legible and easy to read. Pick a font that can be read clearly even when scaled down to a smaller size. Choose a font size that is legible even when viewed from a considerable distance by making the font size large enough. In general, sans-serif fonts are simpler to read than serif fonts, particularly when used at smaller point sizes.

DO NOT: Employ fonts that are difficult to read. It is best to steer clear of using fonts such as script or novelty fonts because they are difficult to read. These fonts can be difficult to read, particularly when they are reduced in size, and using them can give your banner an unprofessional appearance.

DO: Make use of images of a high quality. Make use of images that are both of high quality and pertinent to the point you are trying to make. Make use of images that are both visually appealing and capable of capturing the attention of your audience. Make sure the images you use are optimized for the specific platform that will be displaying your banner.

DO NOT: Use images that are of poor quality or that are not relevant. It is strongly recommended that you refrain from using any images that are pixelated, blurry, or have a low resolution. Your banner may end up looking unprofessional as a result, which will have the effect of making it less effective. Additionally, you should avoid using images that have nothing to do with the audience or the message you are trying to convey. This may cause confusion among your audience and reduce the effectiveness of your banner.

DO: To draw attention to your message, make use of contrasting elements. Make sure that your message is easily recognizable by utilizing contrast in your design. This can be accomplished by making use of color, size, or the positioning of design elements in the layout. Make use of contrast to draw attention to the aspects of your banner that are most important.

DO NOT make use of an excessive amount of colors or contrast. It is best to steer clear of using an excessive amount of colors or contrast, as this can be overpowering and distracting. Maintain a color scheme that is congruent with the identity of your brand, and use contrast sparingly in order to draw attention to the components of your banner that are most significant.

DO: Ensure that your design is optimized for a variety of platforms. Make sure that your banner's design is optimized for the platform that it will be displayed on. This may necessitate the creation of multiple variations of your banner for use across a variety of platforms, including mobile devices, websites, and social media. Check that your design works properly on all of the platforms you intend to use it on.

DO NOT: Implement the same design across all of your platforms. It is best to avoid using the same design for each platform, as each platform has its own specific requirements and limitations. On a website, your banner might look fantastic, but it won't work so well on a mobile device. To ensure that your design has the greatest possible impact, you must first ensure that it is optimized for each platform.

In conclusion, the design of an effective banner needs to incorporate a number of different elements, including readability, simplicity, high-quality images, contrast, and platform optimization. You will be able to create banners that are more visually appealing, effective, and professional-looking in appearance if you follow the dos and don'ts of banner design. This will allow you to achieve better results from your advertising efforts.

# Chapter 6: The Psychology of Color in Banner Advertising

———

B anner advertisements are significantly bolstered by the use of color. Because different colors cause viewers to react emotionally and behaviorally in a variety of ways, it is essential to select colors that are congruent with your brand and the message you want to convey. In this chapter, we will discuss the psychology of color in banner advertising and how you can use it to your advantage. We will also look at how color can be used in other types of advertising.

A sense of excitement, passion, and a sense of the need to act quickly are all associated with the color red. Either to draw attention to important information or to instill a sense of urgency can be accomplished with its use. In sales and promotional banners, the color red is frequently used to encourage viewers to take some kind of action.

Orange is a color that evokes feelings of friendliness, warmth, and zealousness. It is possible to use it to convey a sense of innovation while also giving the impression of playfulness. Banners relating to technology and sports frequently use orange as a primary color.

Yellow is a color that evokes positive emotions such as optimism and happiness, as well as energetic feelings. It is possible to use it to generate a feeling of positivity or to communicate a message of happiness through its use. Banners that are related to food and drink frequently use the color yellow.

The color green is commonly associated with concepts such as prosperity, equilibrium, and the natural world. Either a sense of equilibrium or a message that is kind to the environment can be communicated with its help. Banners that are related to health and wellness frequently use the color green.

There is a strong psychological connection between the color blue and notions of trustworthiness and professionalism. It is possible to use it to convey a message of dependability while also giving the impression of calmness. Banners relating to finance and business frequently make use of the color blue.

The color purple is one that evokes thoughts of opulence, refined elegance, and original thought. It is possible to use it to convey a message of innovation while also giving off an air of sophistication. Banners relating to beauty and fashion frequently make use of the color purple.

There are many connotations attached to the color black, including that of power, sophistication, and elegance. It is possible to generate an atmosphere of luxury with it, as well as communicate a sense of exclusivity through its use. Banners relating to luxury and high-end products frequently use black as their primary color.

White is the color most commonly associated with notions of chastity, simplicity, and purity. It is possible to achieve the effect of minimalism through its use, as well as the effect of purity when communicating with it. Banners that pertain to health and wellness frequently use the color white.

It is essential to keep in mind your company's branding and the message you want to convey when selecting the colors for your banner advertising. It is important that the colors you choose are congruent with the identity of your brand as well as the feelings you want your audience to experience. Make judicious use of color in order to attract attention to vital pieces of information, generate a feeling of imminence, or communicate a message of optimism and trust.

In addition to color, contrast and readability are two additional factors that must be taken into consideration. Make your banner easier to read and draw attention to the information that is most important by using colors that contrast with one another. Be sure that your font is large enough to be easily read, even from a distance, and steer clear of fonts that are difficult to decipher.

In summing up, the psychological impact of color is significant in the role that it plays in banner advertising. You can create banners that are aesthetically pleasing, effective, and emotionally resonant with your audience by selecting colors that align with your branding and messaging, using contrast and readability to make your banner easy to read, and using readability to make your banner easy to understand.

# Chapter 7: A/B Testing Your Banners: Optimizing for Success

In order to have effective banner advertising, the first step is to design a banner that is both aesthetically pleasing and coherent with the message you want to convey. You need to conduct A/B tests on your designs and make adjustments to them in order to truly maximize the effectiveness of your banner. In this chapter, we'll discuss how to conduct A/B testing on your banners and optimize them so that they're more likely to be successful.

A/B testing requires the creation of two versions of your banner, each with a few minor modifications, and then testing them to determine which version is more successful. Using A/B testing, you can determine which aspects of your design will help you achieve your marketing objectives in the most successful manner. The following are some helpful hints for conducting successful A/B tests:

First and foremost, you need to define your marketing goals. It is important to establish your marketing objectives before beginning the A/B testing process. What response are you hoping to elicit from your target audience when they see your banner? Do you want them to make a purchase, sign up for a newsletter, or click on a link that takes them to your website? After you have defined your objectives, you will be able to create designs that are tailored specifically to accomplishing those objectives.

The second piece of advice is to test one variable at a time. It is important to test only one variable at a time when determining the effectiveness of your banner designs in order to get accurate results. This could refer to the color scheme, the "call to action," or even the positioning of design elements. You will be able to determine with greater precision which aspects of the design are most successful if you conduct experiments in which you test one variable at a time and then analyze the results.

Third piece of advice: Be sure to test with a sufficiently large sample size. It is essential to test your banner designs using a sample size that is sufficiently large in order to guarantee accurate results. This entails putting your designs through their paces in front of a demographically representative sample of customers. The larger the number of people in your sample, the more reliable your findings will be.

The fourth piece of advice is to monitor and assess your progress. After you have tried out different designs for your banners, it is critical to monitor and assess how the tests went. Tracking metrics such as click-through rates, conversion rates, and engagement rates requires the utilization of analytics tools. Conduct a thorough analysis of the results to determine which aspects of the design contribute the most to the successful completion of your marketing objectives.

Fifth piece of advice: Polish and perfect your designs. Refine and improve the effectiveness of your banner designs based on the results. This may entail making adjustments to the color scheme, shifting the emphasis of the call to action, or rearranging the positions of various design elements. In order to maximize the impact of your banner, you should continually evaluate and improve its designs.

To summarize, A/B testing is an effective method for improving the effectiveness of your banner advertising. You can create banners that are not only visually appealing but also effective at achieving your marketing goals if you first define your marketing goals, test one variable at a time, test with a sample size that is large enough, track and analyze your results, and then refine and optimize your designs.

# Chapter 8: The Impact of Animation in Banner Advertising

———

B anner advertisements can benefit greatly from the utilization of animation as a tool. Banners that use animation have the ability to hold the attention of viewers while also conveying your message in a manner that is visually interesting. In this chapter, we will discuss the significance of animation in banner advertisements and how you can make the most of its potential benefits.

There are a number of different methods that can be utilized in the production of animated banners, such as animated GIFs, HTML5, and video. The following is a list of ways that animation can have an effect on your banner advertising:

Attention-getting: Animated banners, as opposed to static banners, have a better chance of getting people to pay attention to what they're seeing. Moving images are inherently more interesting to look at and more engaging to interact with than still images, which is why they are more effective at drawing the attention of viewers.

Complex ideas can be conveyed through animation in a way that is both visually engaging and effective in the communication of ideas. You can make your point more clear to viewers and more likely to stick in their memories if you simplify difficult concepts and present them in the form of animations.

Develop an emotional connection with your audience by using animation to develop a connection with them on an emotional level. You can establish a sense of emotional connection with your audience by using animated characters or objects that the viewers can relate to. This type of connection can make it easier for you to motivate your audience to take some kind of action.

Communicate your brand's personality and values in a way that is both visually engaging and effective by using animation to communicate these aspects of your brand. When you bring your brand to life through the use of animation, you give viewers an impression that is more likely to stick with them and have an impact.

Animated banners can increase engagement by encouraging viewers to interact with the banner itself, which in turn increases the amount of time readers spend on the site. This could involve clicking on the banner in order to watch a video or investigate a product in greater depth.

It is essential to keep the following guidelines in mind whenever incorporating animation into banner advertising:

Keep it simple: Avoid using an excessive number of design elements or complex animations, both of which can make the experience too much for viewers or divert their attention. Make sure that your animations are straightforward and that they emphasize the most essential components of your message.

Make use of a distinct call to action: Ensure that your call to action is distinct and easy to spot, even when using animation. Your call to action should benefit from the animation, and it should not hinder its effectiveness.

Take into account the loading times: animated banners typically require more time to load than static banners. If you want your users to have a good experience, you need to make sure that your animation is optimized for quick loading times.

Ensure your animation is in line with your brand's personality and values by making sure it is aligned with your brand. The animation you choose should appear to be a logical continuation of the identity of your brand.

In conclusion, animation has the potential to have a significant impact on the effectiveness of banner advertising. Animation can help make your banners more effective at achieving your marketing goals by drawing attention to them, conveying more complex messages, creating emotional resonance, communicating the personality of your brand, and increasing engagement. When using animation in banner advertising, it is essential to keep the animation straightforward, use a call to action that is unmistakable, take into account loading times, and remain consistent with branding.

# Chapter 9: Maximizing Your ROI: Budgeting for Banner Advertising

———

I t's important to create a budget and use your resources wisely if you want to get the most out of your banner advertising and maximize your return on investment (ROI). Banner advertising is one of the most effective ways to promote your goods or services (ROI). In this chapter, we will discuss how to properly budget for banner advertising in order to maximize your return on investment (ROI).

Determine your objectives: It is important to define your goals for banner advertising before you begin developing a budget for the campaign. Do you want to raise people's awareness of your brand, attract more visitors to your website, or produce more leads and sales? When you define your objectives, it will be easier to decide how much money to put towards banner advertising and which platforms you should concentrate on.

Determine your budget: Once you've nailed down your objectives, the next step is to figure out your financial plan. Think about things like the size of the audience you're trying to reach, how much it costs per impression or click, and how much the whole campaign will set you back. Create a spending plan that will allow you to accomplish all of your objectives without draining all of your available resources.

Choose the appropriate platforms There are a variety of platforms available for banner advertising, some of which include social media, websites, and mobile applications. Choose the platforms that offer the greatest degree of congruence with both the audience you wish to reach and the objectives you wish to achieve with your marketing. Think about things like the demographics of the audience, how popular the platform is, and the various ad format options.

Create a strategy for targeting: Create a strategy for targeting that enables you to reach your ideal audience with your banner ads. Targeting someone based on their demographics, interests, behaviors, or location could be one example of this. If you know your audience well and target them effectively, you can make the most of the money you spend on banner advertising.

Ensure that your banners are optimized for maximum effectiveness by ensuring that they are optimized. You can determine which elements of your banner's design are most effective at achieving your objectives by using A/B testing to compare and contrast the various versions of your banner. In order to maximize the effectiveness of your banners, you should refine and optimize them based on the results of your testing.

Monitor and evaluate your results: Monitor and evaluate your results in order to keep tabs on how far you've come in achieving your marketing objectives. Tracking metrics such as click-through rates, conversion rates, and engagement rates requires the utilization of analytics tools. Conduct a thorough analysis of the results to locate weak spots in your strategy and make the necessary adjustments.

In conclusion, if you want to get the most out of your investment in banner advertising, you need to carefully plan and optimize your budget. You can effectively create effective banner advertising campaigns that deliver results and maximize your marketing budget if you define your goals, determine your budget, choose the appropriate platforms, develop a targeting strategy, optimize your banners, and monitor and analyze your results.

# Chapter 10: Creating a Consistent Brand Identity with Banner Advertising

———

Banner advertising is a powerful tool that can be used to promote your brand and raise awareness of your brand among consumers. It is important to develop a consistent brand identity that resonates with your target audience in order to get the most out of your banner advertising. Banner advertising will be the focus of our discussion in this chapter as we look at how to establish a recognizable brand identity.

Define your brand identity It is important to take the time to define your brand identity before you begin the process of creating banner ads. This encompasses aspects such as the values of your brand, your personality, the tone of your voice, and your visual style. It is important that your company's brand identity is maintained uniformly across all of your different marketing channels, such as your website, social media, and banner ads.

Choose your design elements: Choose design elements such as your color scheme, typography, and imagery that are congruent with your brand identity. This includes your logo. Applying these design principles uniformly across all of your banner ads will help you establish a consistent and easily recognizable brand identity.

Maintain a tone of voice that is consistent throughout: Maintain a tone of voice throughout your banner ads that is consistent with your brand's personality. This could mean being lighthearted, profound, educational, or even emotionally charged. Your brand identity can be strengthened by maintaining a consistent tone of voice, and it can also help viewers form an impression that is more likely to stick with them.

Ensure that your marketing goals and your banner ads are aligned. Ensure that your marketing goals and your banner ads are aligned. This entails centering your attention on the advantages offered by your goods or services and putting an emphasis on the problems that they solve for your target audience. Make use of messaging that is both relatable to your intended audience and congruent with the identity of your brand.

Optimize for multiple platforms Make sure that your banner ads are optimized for multiple platforms, including social media, websites, and mobile applications. This necessitates giving thought to the dimensions of your banner ads, as well as the structure and composition of their designs, in order to guarantee that they appear attractive and are successful across all platforms.

Test and improve: Run multiple iterations of your banner ads to determine which aspects of their design contribute the most to meeting your marketing objectives, then refine those aspects as necessary. Refine your banner ads based on the results of your testing to increase their efficiency and solidify the connection between your brand and the consumer.

To summarize, it is essential to develop a consistent brand identity through the use of banner advertising if you want to raise awareness of your brand and resound with your target audience. Create a cohesive and memorable brand identity that connects with your target audience and drives results for your business by defining your brand identity, selecting your design elements, using a consistent tone of voice, aligning with your marketing goals, optimizing for different platforms, and testing and refining your banner ads. This can be accomplished by defining your brand identity, choosing your design elements, using a consistent tone of voice, and aligning with your marketing goals.

# Chapter 11: The Mobile Revolution: Designing Banners for Mobile Devices

———

It is more important than ever before to design banners that are optimized for viewing on mobile devices due to the rise in popularity of mobile devices. Because of the different screen sizes, resolutions, and user behaviors associated with mobile devices, a different strategy is required for the design of banners. In this chapter, we'll take a look at how banners can be designed in such a way that they are compatible with mobile devices.

Keep it simple: Because mobile screens are smaller than desktop screens, it is essential that the design of your banner be kept straightforward and concentrated. Employ a message that is uncomplicated, unambiguous, and emphatic in its call to action. When designing for a smaller screen, try to avoid using too many design elements or chunks of text that may be difficult to read.

Utilize a design that is responsive: Utilize a design that is responsive, which adjusts itself to different screen sizes and resolutions. This ensures that your banner will have an excellent appearance on any mobile device, regardless of whether it is a smartphone or a tablet. Make sure that the design of your banner can be viewed effectively on a variety of mobile devices.

Make use of images of a high quality: Make use of images of a high quality that have been optimized for mobile devices. It is important that images have a high resolution and are optimized so that they load quickly. Images should also be pertinent to the message being conveyed by the banner as well as its design.

Mobile users interact with banners in a different way than desktop users do, so it's important to optimize for touch. Make sure that your banner is optimized for touch by adding features such as larger buttons and navigation that is simple to use. Employ a call to action that is unambiguous, easy to understand, and quick to click on from a mobile device.

Put your banner design to the test: Put your banner design to the test on a variety of mobile devices to ensure that it not only looks great but is also simple to use. For the purpose of determining how successful your banner design is, you should make use of analytics tools to track metrics such as click-through rates and engagement rates.

In conclusion, designing banners for mobile devices requires a different approach than designing banners for desktop screens. This is because mobile devices do not have the same screen real estate as desktop computers. You can create banners that are optimized for mobile viewing and effective at achieving your marketing goals by keeping your design simple, utilizing a responsive design, using high-quality images, optimizing for touch, and testing your banner design.

# Chapter 12: Targeting Your Audience: Strategies for Effective Banner Placement

———

When it comes to the success of your banner advertising campaign, banner placement is one of the most important factors. Banner placement that is done correctly ensures that your banner will be seen by your target audience, which can lead to an increase in engagement as well as conversions. In this chapter, we will discuss effective banner placement strategies, as well as techniques for focusing on a specific audience.

Before you begin to place your banners, it is important to make sure that you have a solid understanding of the people who will be viewing them. This encompasses aspects such as their demographics, interests, behaviors, and location among other things. Make use of this information to determine the locations in which your audience will be most likely to see your banner and engage with it.

Pick the right platforms: When deciding which platforms to use, pick the ones that are the best fit for both your intended audience and the objectives you want to achieve with your marketing. Think about things like the demographics of the audience, how popular the platform is, and the various ad format options. This may include mobile applications, websites, and social media platforms.

Put your banner ads on websites or apps that are relevant to your target audience by making use of contextual targeting. This can be accomplished through the use of keyword targeting or topic targeting, both of which involve matching your banner ads with content that is relevant to the subject matter.

Utilize retargeting. Retargeting enables you to display your banner ads to people who have already interacted with your website or other marketing materials in the past. Targeting individuals who are already familiar with your brand is one way to boost the efficiency of your banner ads.

Take into account the placement of your banner ads within the platform. Take into account the placement of your banner ads within the platform. For instance, elevating your banner advertisement to a more visible position, such as at the very top of a web page, can boost both its visibility and the amount of engagement it receives.

Adapt your website to mobile users by adapting your banner ads to work properly on mobile devices such as smartphones and tablets. This means making use of a design that is responsive and adapts itself to a variety of screen sizes and resolutions.

Experiment and refine: Try out a variety of different banner placements, and then look at the results to see which placements were the most successful in helping you achieve your marketing objectives. In order to get the most out of your campaign, you should adjust your strategy for banner placement based on the results of your testing.

To summarize, proper banner placement is critical to successfully targeting your audience and accomplishing your marketing objectives. You can develop a successful banner advertising campaign that generates results by first gaining an understanding of the demographics of your target audience, then selecting the appropriate platforms, utilizing contextual targeting and retargeting, thinking about ad placement, optimizing for mobile, testing and refining your strategy, and finally, putting it all together.

# Chapter 13: The Power of Social Media Advertising with Banners

———

A dvertising on social media platforms is quickly becoming one of the most common and widely used strategies for promoting businesses and products on the internet. Businesses are able to reach a large audience in a way that is visually engaging through the use of banner advertising, which is a powerful tool for the advertising of social media. In this chapter, we will discuss the effectiveness of using banner ads when advertising on social media.

Make sure you use the appropriate platform: Pick the social media platform that best fits the marketing goals you want to achieve and the audience you want to reach. The demographics of the users, their interests, and their behaviors all vary depending on the platform. Banner advertisements are seen frequently on Facebook, Instagram, Twitter, and LinkedIn, which are all examples of popular social media platforms.

Utilize a design that is responsive: Utilize a design that is responsive, which adjusts itself to different screen sizes and resolutions. This will ensure that your banner appears beautifully on all devices, including mobile phones, tablets, and desktop computers.

Make sure your messaging and imagery are crystal clear. Make sure your messaging and imagery are crystal clear, and make sure it aligns with the identity of your brand and resonates with the audience you're trying to reach. Your message and the benefits it offers should be communicated in a manner that is clear, concise, and visually appealing via your banner.

Utilize retargeting. Retargeting enables you to display your banner ads to people who have already interacted with your website or other marketing materials in the past. Targeting individuals who are already familiar with your brand is one way to boost the efficiency of your banner ads.

Experiment with different banner designs, messaging, and platforms to see which one helps you achieve your marketing goals more effectively. Then, refine your approach based on what you've learned. To get the most out of your campaign, you should adjust your approach in light of the results of your testing.

Utilize the targeting capabilities of social media: Utilize the targeting capabilities of social media in order to reach your ideal audience based on demographics, interests, behaviors, and location. This ensures that the individuals who are most likely to interact with your brand are exposed to your banner advertisements.

Utilize video banners to effectively engage your audience and communicate your message in a way that is visually engaging. Video banners are an effective way to engage your audience. Utilize videos of high quality that have been optimized for quick loading times, and communicate your message in a way that is succinct while also being visually engaging.

In conclusion, advertising on social media through the use of banners can be an extremely efficient way to promote your company and its products on the internet. You can create an effective social media advertising campaign that resonates with your target audience and accomplishes your marketing goals by selecting the appropriate platform, using a responsive design, using clear messaging and imagery, using retargeting, testing and refining your strategy, using social media targeting, and using video banners. If you do this, you will be able to create a powerful social media advertising campaign.

# Chapter 14: Measuring Your Success: Analytics and Metrics for Banner Advertising

———

It is essential to measure the success of your banner advertising campaign if you want to maximize its efficiency and make progress toward your marketing objectives. You are able to track the performance of your banner ads with the help of analytics and metrics, which enables you to identify areas for improvement and refine your strategy. In the following section, we will discuss analytics and metrics pertaining to banner advertising.

The number of times that users have seen your banner advertisement is referred to as the impressions your ad has received. This metric gives you an idea of how far your banner advertisement campaign has been seen.

Click-through rate, also known as CTR, is calculated by dividing the total number of clicks your banner ad has received by the total number of times it has been displayed. This metric gives you an indication of how successful your banner ad is at generating interest and engagement among your target audience.

Conversion rate: A website's conversion rate can be calculated by dividing the number of users who completed a desired action, such as making a purchase or filling out a form, by the total number of clicks on the website. This metric gives an indication of how effective your banner ad is at driving conversions by providing information about how many people have clicked on it.

The number of interactions with your banner ad, such as clicks, likes, comments, and shares, is referred to as the engagement rate, and it is calculated by dividing the total number of impressions by the total number of interactions. This metric gives you an indication of how engaged your audience is with your banner ad and provides you with that information over time.

The cost of each click on your banner ad is referred to as the cost per click, abbreviated CPC for short. This metric is essential for gaining an understanding of the cost-effectiveness of the banner advertising campaign you are running.

Return on investment (ROI) is the term used to describe the amount of profit you made from the money you put into your banner advertising campaign. This metric takes both the cost of your campaign as well as the revenue that was generated from it into consideration. This metric gives you an idea of how successful your campaign has been in general.

Analytics can also provide information on the demographics of your audience, such as their age, gender, location, and interests. This information can be gleaned from your audience's age, gender, and interests. This information can be put to use to further hone your targeting and produce banner ads that are more successful.

In conclusion, analytics and metrics are indispensable tools for determining whether or not your banner advertising campaign was successful. You can gain insights into the effectiveness of your campaign and further refine your strategy to achieve your marketing goals if you track impressions, CTR, conversion rate, engagement rate, cost per click (CPC), return on investment (ROI), and demographics of your audience.

# Chapter 15: The Future of Banner Advertising: Trends and Predictions

⸻

In recent years, banner advertising has undergone a significant transformation, which has been driven by developments in technology as well as shifting user behaviors. There are a number of current trends as well as future predictions that are likely to have an effect on the future of banner advertising. In this chapter, we will investigate the foreseeable future of banner advertising and the implications that this trend has for companies.

Personalization: Banner advertising is not an exception to the rule that personalization is becoming an increasingly important aspect of digital marketing. Through the use of personalization, businesses are able to generate banner advertisements that are better targeted and more relevant to their audience.

Banners that allow users to interact with the banner in a meaningful way are growing in popularity, and as a result, interactive banners are becoming increasingly common. This may involve the use of animations, games, quizzes, and other forms of interactivity that boost engagement and drive results.

Artificial intelligence (AI): AI is increasingly being incorporated into digital marketing, and banner advertising is not an exception to this trend. Artificial intelligence can be applied to the analysis of data and the optimization of banner ads in real time, enabling businesses to develop more successful marketing campaigns.

The technology behind augmented reality (AR) is becoming more widely available, and it is likely to become more integrated into banner advertising. Users are able to interact with the banner in a more immersive manner using augmented reality (AR), which increases engagement and drives results.

Voice search: It is likely that, as voice search becomes more popular, banner advertising will become increasingly integrated into the results of voice search. Because of this, companies will need to optimize their banner ads for voice search queries in order to ensure that they appear in search results that are relevant to their products or services.

Design for mobile devices first: As the use of mobile devices continues to rise, banner advertisements will need to be designed with mobile devices as the primary focus. This requires the production of banner advertisements with a design that is responsive to mobile devices, as well as clear and concise messaging and visually appealing content.

Data privacy: Because of the increased focus on data privacy, businesses will need to be more open and honest about the ways in which they collect and use customers' personal information. This necessitates the provision of information that is unambiguous and concise regarding the collection and utilization of data, as well as the granting of users control over the data that pertains to them.

In conclusion, personalization, interactive banners, artificial intelligence, augmented reality, voice search, mobile-first design, and data privacy are likely to play significant roles in the development of the future of banner advertising. Businesses that are able to adjust to these trends and that are willing to embrace new technologies and methods will be in the best position to be successful in the future of banner advertising.

# Chapter 16: Beyond the Banner: Exploring Alternative Forms of Digital Advertising

———

Even though banner advertising is still one of the most common and successful types of digital advertising, there are a variety of other types of digital advertising that companies can investigate. These nontraditional modes of advertising may provide distinctive advantages as well as fresh opportunities to interact with audiences in a variety of novel ways. In the following section, we will investigate some additional options for digital advertising that are open to consideration by businesses.

Native advertising is a form of advertising that is designed to blend in with the content that is surrounding it. This makes native advertising less intrusive and more engaging for the audience because it appears less out of place. The use of sponsored content, product placement, or article recommendations are all examples of native advertising formats.

Influencer marketing is a form of marketing that involves forming partnerships with people who have a large following on social media in order to promote products or services. Influencers typically have a dedicated fan base and are an efficient means of communicating with specific target audiences.

Video advertising: Video advertising has become increasingly popular over the past few years, driven in large part by the rise in popularity of websites and platforms such as YouTube and social media sites that feature video content. There are a few different formats for video advertisements, including pre-roll ads, in-stream ads, and sponsored content.

Email marketing is a form of digital marketing that entails sending promotional messages to a list of customers who have opted in to receive them. Email marketing has the potential to be very efficient when it comes to reaching repeat customers and generating conversions.

Search engine marketing (SEM) refers to the process of optimizing your website and developing targeted advertisements to be displayed on the result pages of search engines. Reaching customers who are already interested in purchasing your goods or services can be made significantly easier with search engine optimization (SEM).

Advertising on social media: advertising on social media entails promoting your goods or services on social media websites such as Facebook, Twitter, and Instagram. Advertising on social media can be extremely targeted and therefore very effective when trying to reach specific niche audiences.

In programmatic advertising, software is used to automatically buy and sell digital advertising inventory. This type of advertising is known as programmatic advertising. Advertisements that are targeted to specific audiences using programmatic methods can be extremely efficient and effective.

In conclusion, in addition to banner advertising, there are a variety of other forms of digital advertising that companies can investigate. Businesses have the ability to broaden their audience reach, engage with audiences in new ways, and accomplish their marketing goals by taking into consideration advertising strategies such as native advertising, influencer marketing, video advertising, email marketing, search engine marketing, social media advertising, and programmatic advertising.

# Chapter 17: Case Studies: Success Stories in Banner Advertising

—————

B anner advertising has been used by companies of all sizes and in all kinds of industries to reach new audiences and accomplish their marketing objectives. In the following section, we will investigate several case studies of successful banner advertising campaigns.

Airbnb: In order to promote its vacation rental service on social media websites such as Facebook and Instagram, Airbnb utilized banner advertisements. Banner advertisements featured high-quality images of one-of-a-kind and interesting places to stay, along with a call-to-action directing potential guests to make a reservation. A 300% increase in bookings was achieved as a direct result of the campaign.

Banner advertisements were utilized by HubSpot in order to promote its inbound marketing platform on LinkedIn. The messaging in the banner ads was straightforward and easy to understand, and they included a prompt encouraging readers to find out more. The campaign was successful in that it brought about a 650% increase in leads.

Banner advertisements were utilized by Dropbox in order to promote its file sharing and storage service on various social media websites such as Facebook and Twitter. The banner ads had enticing visuals and concise messaging, in addition to a call to action encouraging users to sign up for a free trial of the service. The campaign led to a rise in signups that was 400% higher than expected.

Banner advertisements were utilized by Chevrolet in order to promote the 2017 Bolt EV on mobile devices. An interactive quiz that tested users' knowledge about electric vehicles and a call-to-action to learn more about the Bolt EV were both included in the banner ads that were displayed on the website. The campaign led to a three hundred percent increase in the number of test drive requests.

Banner ads were utilized by Squarespace in order to promote its website builder across various social media platforms including Facebook and Instagram. The banner ads contained enticing visuals and concise messaging, as well as a call to action encouraging users to begin the process of building a website. The campaign led to a three hundred percent increase in the number of signups.

In conclusion, these case studies show that banner advertising is powerful and effective for accomplishing marketing goals. Businesses are able to develop successful banner advertising campaigns that drive results by utilizing engaging visuals, clear messaging, and a powerful call to action in their advertisements.

# Chapter 18: Creative Inspiration: Exploring the Best Banner Designs

---

B anner advertising is a highly visual medium; therefore, creative design is essential to the production of effective banner advertisements that strike a chord with audiences. In this chapter, we will look at some of the most creative and inspiring banner designs that have been created over the years.

The "Just Do It" advertising campaign that was run by Nike is a prime example of successful banner advertising. The banner ads have designs that are bold and minimalistic, with simple messaging that is meant to resonate with the audience that the brand is trying to reach.

Coca-Cola: The banner ads for Coca-Cola feature eye-catching visuals and playful messaging, both of which reinforce the brand's image as a fun and joyful one. The audience's attention can be captured and an emotional connection can be established by employing imagery that is both interesting and visually striking.

Apple: Apple's banner ads have designs that are clean and sophisticated, and they put the emphasis on the features and benefits of the product. The creation of a sense of luxury and sophistication that is closely associated with the brand is accomplished through the utilization of clean lines, white space, and high-quality product images.

Google: The banner ads on Google are famous for their wit and their ability to keep things simple. The banner ads have humorous illustrations and clever messaging that reinforce the brand's reputation for being approachable and friendly to customers.

McDonald's: McDonald's banner ads feature designs that are bright and bold, and they include images of the brand's products that make your mouth water. A sense of excitement and urgency is created for viewers of the advertisement, which encourages them to go to a McDonald's restaurant. This sense is created through the use of simple messaging and colorful visuals.

Old Spice: The banner ads for Old Spice feature a combination of humor and masculinity that speaks to the brand's target audience in a way that is resonant with them. The banner ads have eye-catching designs that are quirky and bold, and they feature witty messaging that reinforces the brand's image as a brand for men that is fun and confident.

Airbnb: The banner ads of Airbnb feature stunning photographs of one-of-a-kind and interesting vacation rentals, along with a call to action to book a stay at one of these rentals. The utilization of high-quality images and engaging messaging helps to generate an atmosphere of excitement and adventure, which in turn encourages viewers to investigate the possibilities presented by Airbnb.

In conclusion, in order for banner advertising to be effective, the design must be creative in a way that resonates with audiences and reinforces the image and messaging of the brand. Businesses are able to create effective banner advertisements that grab the attention of their audience, create emotional connections, and drive results by researching the best banner designs and drawing inspiration from campaigns that have been successful in the past.

# Chapter 19: Navigating the Complex World of Banner Advertising Regulations

---

Banner advertising is subject to a variety of regulations and guidelines that are designed to protect consumers and ensure fair competition. These regulations and guidelines are designed to protect consumers and ensure fair competition. Although navigating these regulations can be difficult at times, it is essential for businesses to do so in order to avoid legal complications and reputational damage. When it comes to creating and managing banner advertising campaigns, companies need to be aware of a number of important regulations and guidelines. We'll discuss some of these important regulations and guidelines in this chapter.

Guidelines provided by the Federal Trade Commission (FTC) The Federal Trade Commission offers guidelines for various forms of online advertising, including banner ads. These guidelines require companies to avoid making deceptive or misleading claims in their advertisements and to disclose any material connections or endorsements that they have received.

In accordance with the Children's Online Privacy Protection Act (COPPA), businesses are required to obtain the consent of a child's parent or legal guardian before collecting personally identifiable information from children younger than 13 years old. This is true for all advertisements on banners that are aimed at children.

General Data Protection Regulation (GDPR): The GDPR is a regulation that was passed by the European Union that mandates businesses obtain the express consent of individuals before collecting, storing, or using the personal data of those individuals. This is true for advertisements on banners that are directed toward people living in the EU.

principles of self-regulation offered by the Digital Advertising Alliance (DAA) The Digital Advertising Alliance (DAA) offers principles of self-regulation for online advertising, including banner ads. Under these principles, businesses are obligated to provide customers with information and options regarding the collection and use of their data, as well as to comply with the most effective data collection and use standards in the industry.

Restrictions on the content of advertisements Banner advertisements may be subject to certain content restrictions, such as those pertaining to alcoholic beverages, tobacco products, gambling, or adult-oriented content. It is important for companies to be aware of these restrictions and make sure that their advertisements do not violate any laws or regulations that may be in effect.

Legislation pertaining to intellectual property Banner advertisements may be subject to legislation pertaining to intellectual property, such as that which governs infringement of copyright or trademarks. Companies have a responsibility to ensure that their advertisements do not violate the intellectual property rights of third parties.

In conclusion, in order for businesses to successfully navigate the complicated world of banner advertising regulations, they need to ensure that they are up to date on relevant information and that they comply with all relevant laws and guidelines. Businesses are able to avoid legal issues and reputational damage while creating effective banner advertising campaigns if they understand and adhere to regulations related to the Federal Trade Commission (FTC), the Children's Online Privacy Protection Act (COPPA), the General Data Protection Regulation (GDPR), the Digital Advertising Alliance (DAA), and laws pertaining to intellectual property.

# Chapter 20: Mastering the Art of Banner Advertising: Tips from Top Industry Experts

———

Because banner advertising is a complex field that is always evolving, it can be difficult for businesses to keep up with the most recent trends and strategies. Banner advertising is a skill that can be learned, and fortunately, there are many professionals in the field who can provide insightful advice and suggestions. In this chapter, we will discuss some of the best advice for developing successful banner advertising campaigns that has been provided by professionals in the industry.

Chief Executive Officer of DigitalMarketer, Ryan Deiss: "Banner ads benefit greatly from having distinct calls to action. Make it abundantly clear what you want the viewer to do next, whether it is to make a purchase, sign up for a newsletter, or click through to your website."

As the founder of Neil Patel Digital, Neil Patel says the following: "Concentrate on producing eye-catching visuals of a high quality that will capture the attention of the viewer. Make your banner ad stand out from the crowd by employing striking colors, captivating imagery, and concise messaging."

Rand Fishkin, the man who founded Moz: "You shouldn't be afraid to try out a variety of placements and formats for your advertisements. Experiment with a variety of different layouts, sizes, and targeting options to determine what will work best for your company."

MarketingProfs' Chief Content Officer Ann Handley says the following: "Make it a priority to design banner ads that provide the viewer with information and are helpful to them. Offer something of value to your audience in the form of instructive content, practical advice, or useful resources."

MobileMonkey's Chief Executive Officer, Larry Kim: "Ensure that your banner advertisement is compatible with mobile devices. If you want your advertisement to look great and be easy to interact with on mobile devices, you should use a design that is responsive and communicates clearly."

The following is a statement made by Jay Baer, the company's founder: "Retargeting should be a component of the banner advertising strategy that you employ. Retargeting enables you to display advertisements to users who have already engaged with your brand or visited your website, thereby increasing the likelihood of a conversion taking place."

Avinash Kaushik, digital marketing evangelist at Google: "Concentrate on important metrics such as return on investment and conversion rate. Make use of analytics to monitor how well your banner ads are performing, and adjust your strategy in light of what is and is not producing the desired results."

In conclusion, becoming an expert in the art of banner advertising calls for a combination of creative thinking, a willingness to experiment, and an understanding of how to draw insights from data. Businesses are able to create effective banner advertising campaigns that drive results and achieve their marketing goals by following the tips and advice provided by top industry experts such as Ryan Deiss, Neil Patel, Rand Fishkin, Ann Handley, Larry Kim, Jay Baer, and Avinash Kaushik.

# Also by B. Vincent

**Affiliate Marketing**
Affiliate Marketing
Affiliate Marketing

**Standalone**
Business Employee Discipline
Affiliate Recruiting
Business Layoffs & Firings
Business and Entrepreneur Guide
Business Remote Workforce
Career Transition
Project Management
Precision Targeting
Professional Development
Strategic Planning
Content Marketing
Imminent List Building
Getting Past GateKeepers
Banner Ads
Bookkeeping
Bridge Pages
Business Acquisition

Business Bogging
Business Communication Course
Marketing Automation
Better Meetings
Business Conflict Resolution
Business Culture Course
Conversion Optimization
Creative Solutions
Employee Recruitment
Startup Capital
Employee Incentives
Employee Mentoring
Followership
Servant Leadership
Human Resources
Team Building
Freelancing
Funnel Building
Geo Targeting
Goal Setting
Immanent List Building
Lead Generation
Leadership Course
Leadership Transition
Leadership vs Management
LinkedIn Ads
LinkedIn Marketing
Messenger Marketing
New Management
Newsfeed Ads
Search Ads
Online Learning
Sales Webinars

# About the Publisher

Accepting manuscripts in the most categories. We love to help people get their words available to the world.

Revival Waves of Glory focus is to provide more options to be published. We do traditional paperbacks, hardcovers, audio books and ebooks all over the world. A traditional royalty-based publisher that offers self-publishing options, Revival Waves provides a very author friendly and transparent publishing process, with President Bill Vincent involved in the full process of your book. Send us your manuscript and we will contact you as soon as possible.

Contact: Bill Vincent at rwgpublishing@yahoo.com